HOW TO BE A

GAMING
INFLUENCER

ANITA NAHTA AMIN

raintree

a Capstone company — publishers for children

Raintree is an imprint of Capstone Global Library Limited, a company incorporated in England and Wales having its registered office at 264 Banbury Road, Oxford, OX2 7DY – Registered company number: 6695582

www.raintree.co.uk
myorders@raintree.co.uk

Edited by Peter Mavrikis
Designed by Brann Garvey
Original illustrations © Capstone Global Library Limited 2022
Picture research by Morgan Walters
Production by Tori Abraham
Originated by Capstone Global Library Ltd

978 1 3982 1553 5 (hardback)
978 1 3982 1577 1 (paperback)

British Library Cataloguing in Publication Data
A full catalogue record for this book is available from the British Library.

Acknowledgements
We would like to thank the following for permission to reproduce photographs: Getty Images: Andrew Benge, 7; iStockphoto: Brankospejs, 18, ilbusca, 11, ohishiistk, 34, PhotoAttractive, 22, supersizer, 38; Newscom: FIRST NATIONAL, 35, Jens Wolf/dpa/picture-alliance, 15; Shutterstock: Afizkes, 9, AhmadBrutalism666, 17, Alex SG, 12, Anterovium, Cover design element throughout, Anton27, 4, aslysun, 39, Atmosphere1, 14, Casezy idea, 21, Dragana Gordic, 27, Ekaterina_Minaeva, 31, Epov Dmitry, 16, everydayplus, 37, Gal Istvan Gal, 41, GaudiLab, 25, karnoff, Cover (icons), kristinasavkov, Cover (controller), Omnart, Cover (thumb up), Prostock-studio, 44, Rawpixel.com, 29, Roman Kosolapov, 10, 43, Stokkete, 32, vichie81, 30.

Every effort has been made to contact copyright holders of material reproduced in this book. Any omissions will be rectified in subsequent printings if notice is given to the publisher.

All the internet addresses (URLs) given in this book were valid at the time of going to press. However, due to the dynamic nature of the internet, some addresses may have changed, or sites may have changed or ceased to exist since publication. While the author and publisher regret any inconvenience this may cause readers, no responsibility for any such changes can be accepted by either the author or the publisher.

CONTENTS

Words in **bold** are in the glossary.

WATCH ME PLAY!

Lights, camera, action! Your spaceship lurches forwards. You dodge asteroids, alien attacks and solar flares. But a black hole looms ahead. It's sucking you towards it! Every button on your navigator board lights up. Your systems are failing! Luckily, you've earned a spare energy blaster. It will power your ship back up! Millions of people watch you narrowly escape the black hole. You safely land on Mars and move up to the next level.

All the while you've been narrating your adventure to your social media fans as you play this new video game. Even better, you've earned money doing it – as a gaming social influencer.

CHAPTER 1

WHAT IS A GAMING INFLUENCER?

"This is so cool!" Have you ever hyped up a video game? Did a friend catch your excitement and want to play too? Or maybe you didn't like the game, so your friend didn't either.

Gaming influencers affect the decision-making of their "friends" too. Influencers share their thoughts through online **social media**. They showcase their favourite games and trends through videos, posts and **livestreaming**. Their fans may try a game after watching a video. In fact, more than 82 per cent of fans buy a product based on what an influencer says.

Fast Fact!

While online, most people watch videos over any other form of content.

Ethan Gamer, here 11 years old, has even created his own mobile game!

Influencers can have more sway and fans than film stars! At the age of seven, British influencer Ethan Gamer started posting online videos about his favourite games. Now he has millions of fans, and his content has been viewed more than one billion times.

An online audience

Influencers span all ages and countries. The number of child influencers, or "kidfluencers", keeps growing. Fans can sign up on social media as online followers of an influencer. Following makes it easier for a fan to keep track of new content to watch.

Influencers are often grouped by follower count. People may define the levels differently, but the lowest is usually a nano-influencer. They have fewer than 10,000 followers. The highest is a macro-influencer with more than 1 million. Celebrities are often macro-influencers.

Influencer levels

Number of followers	Influencer
< 10,000	Nano
10,000–100,000	Micro
100,000–1 million	Mid-level
> 1 million	Macro

Business or play?

Influencers – including children – can become millionaires! The gaming market is worth more than £108 billion. Game makers pay influencers millions of pounds a year to advertise games.

Before smartphones became common, most adverts were on television. Now, many people spend time online instead. So more game makers are turning to influencers to advertise games online. If you're not a gamer, though, don't worry! Game brands also reach out to non-gamers to grow their customer base.

Influencers can reach thousands, or even millions, of online fans.

Influencing isn't just fun and games. It's often a business. Influencers make business deals. They file reports on what they earned and spent. They set schedules. They are more than just social media stars.

Gaming influencers review games, teach strategy and more. They might play for fun or be pros. Some play on **e-sports** teams. These are similar to basketball or football teams, but the sport is video games.

Fans cheer on gamers at an e-sports event.

Early E-sports Tournaments

Space games starred in some of the first e-sports contests. Winners got small prizes such as magazines and games. In 1972, students at the US university of Stanford wanted to know who was best at a rocket ship game. So they held the Intergalactic Spacewar Olympics. Later, in 1980, game maker Atari held the Space Invaders Championship. This time, 10,000 players showed up to fight space aliens.

Space Invaders was a popular game on the Atari 2600 console.

Game makers host flashy e-sports tournaments to excite and bring together fans and influencers. Hundreds of teams compete for multi-million pound prizes. Millions of worldwide fans root for their favourite e-sports team in an arena or online. Some e-sports events have larger audiences than professional sports teams. Large companies work with e-sports teams and players to advertise during events.

CHAPTER 2

GETTING STARTED

Are you ready to become the next Ethan Gamer?
If so, remember to be yourself! People follow authentic
influencers who feel like trusted friends. A million
people probably won't follow you at once, so be patient.
It may take a few years to earn any money.

Have a plan

To prepare, decide whether to focus on one type of game or more. Do you like sports? Adventures? Puzzles? Different games attract different audiences. Some games are played online. Some use a **console** or a gaming PC. Some are less commonly played at arcades. Mobile games are the most popular. Most need to connect to the internet, but they can be played anywhere on devices such as a smartphone or tablet.

Make sure you check your game instructions and licence. Some don't allow sharing of game content. If you do share, you're breaking **copyright** laws.

The world's first video game?

OXO was a tic-tac-toe game built in 1952. But it lacked moving pictures on a screen, so some people say it wasn't a real video game. *Tennis for Two* was built in 1958. It had moving graphics. But it didn't use a video signal to make the images, so some people say it wasn't a real video game. There is still debate on what a video game is and which one was the world's first.

Learn about the influencer and gaming markets. Read agency blogs such as MediaKix and gaming magazines such as *110% Gaming*. Follow your favourite gamers on social media to see how they work. You could even attend influencer training camps, though these may cost hundreds of pounds.

What will you play? Will you keep it old school with arcade games or try the hottest new mobile games?

Ralph Baer poses in 2009 with the Brown Box.

Ralph Baer, the father of video games

As a child, Ralph Baer and his family fled to New York, USA, from Germany just before the start of World War II. He worked in a factory and saved money to take a class on how to fix televisions. Many years later, in the late 1960s, he made the world's first video game console. The "Brown Box" let multiple users play games on a TV. The box had a row of switches on the front to choose the game. His inventions are now in museums, and in 2006, then-President George W. Bush awarded him a National Medal of Technology.

Create your brand

An influencer often presents themselves as a brand. What is your brand? It's you – your personality, tone and message. Are you serious or funny, shy or outgoing? What message do you want your followers to take away? These are questions to think about before you start making content.

Many gamers use a **logo**. This is a symbol to catch people's attention and help them remember your brand. Ethan Gamer's logo is a head with earphones and his initials. You can make a logo using an online logo maker, some of which charge a fee. Many gamers

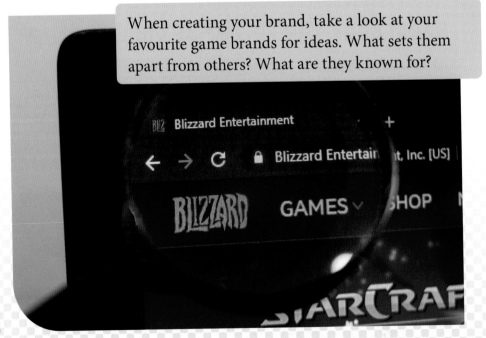

When creating your brand, take a look at your favourite game brands for ideas. What sets them apart from others? What are they known for?

A logo should be simple but unique. When people see it, they should know it's yours!

play under a "gamertag" or nickname too. Like a logo, a gamertag helps people identify you from thousands of other influencers.

Setting up a personal website can help showcase your brand. It acts as a central link to everything you have online. Ask an adult to help pick a website host to register your website address. The host may charge a few pounds a month. But you can use their tools – or pay a professional – to build your website. On your site, include a biography to introduce yourself. Viewers often check biographies before deciding to follow someone.

Stand out from the crowd

It's easy to get lost in a crowd of influencers. To
stand out, think about what you want to be known
for. Demonstrating the latest game? Coaching other
gamers? Crafting your own games? Find your hook.
Your content should be different and useful so
followers crave more.

Teaming up with other influencers and brand companies can increase your visibility. Their followers may follow you too. For a fee, **agents** work to connect influencers to game brands and other types of brands. Gamers can advertise more than just games. For example, everyone needs toothpaste, whether they play games or not. The agent fee is a percentage of influencer income – typically 10 per cent.

Using **hashtags** makes your content easier to find. Users filter posts by using hashtags. Behind the scenes, a computer program runs a formula to pick which posts show up first. The formula changes a lot. It is based on your content, views, likes, how much you post, how many people you follow and more.

Fast Fact!

Playing video games helps the mind with memory and attention. But too much play injures hands and can affect the user's mood.

Set up shop

Before you create content, make sure you have the right equipment. Decide on a workspace. Perhaps you have a favourite place at home. Check the room for proper lighting or buy a lighting kit. Make sure the space is big enough and quiet for filming.

You'll need a computer and internet connection for online tasks. You can use a smartphone or webcam for photos and films, or buy a camera or camcorder. Many influencers use tripods to hold their cameras steady and microphones for better sound quality. In addition to your gaming device, special computer programs and parts may be needed to livestream, film and edit videos. Some of these tools are free, while others cost hundreds of pounds.

Fast Fact!

Take your pick: National Video Games Day is 12 September, but National Video Game Day is 8 July!

Equipment needed

- Computer
- Internet connection
- Gaming device
- Video camera
- Livestreaming software/hardware
- Film editing software
- Light kit (optional)
- Tripod (optional)
- Microphone (optional)

Build a team

It can take hours to film, edit and upload videos. Will you work with other gamers? Will someone, including adults, help you? Their time and yours have value – even if money isn't traded. **Human capital** is measured as worker talent and labour time. Assigning work based on each person's strengths may help efficiency and **economics**.

Choose your social media platforms

Gaming influencers often use some or all of these platforms: Twitch, YouTube and Instagram. Twitch is for livestreaming game play or e-sports. YouTube runs videos up to 12 hours long, which makes it ideal for game highlights, walkthroughs and more. Instagram supports photos and videos as long as an hour. It works well for quick gaming tips.

All three platforms offer special perks when an influencer reaches a certain follower count or other milestone. These features include extra tools to study follower engagement and earn money. On YouTube and Instagram, you can set up business accounts that let you use similar tools right away. Twitch doesn't have separate business accounts. Instead, Twitch charges a monthly fee. The higher the fee you pay, the more perks you get.

To set up your accounts, you'll need an email address. YouTube requires a Google account too. Children younger than 13 years old must have their parent or guardian's consent, and the adult must help run the account. To use Twitch, children must be at least age 13 and need parental consent up to age 18.

Fast Fact!
On 23 April 2005, the first YouTube video was posted. It was filmed at San Diego Zoo, USA.

Consider being active on multiple social media platforms. Technology changes quickly and platforms vanish. Vine was popular for 6-second videos but it closed in 2016, stranding many influencers. New platforms can become the new favourites. Then *poof* – your followers disappear unless you switch too. Power cuts and hackers have shut down platforms for days. Being active on multiple platforms provides a backup if one fails and may help you gain followers.

Social media platforms

Instagram
- Photos
- Videos up to 1 minute
- Instagram IGTV – videos ranging 1 minute to 1 hour, as well as series
- Instagram Stories – temporary slideshow of photos and videos

YouTube
- Videos up to 12 hours

Twitch
- Livestreams

Build a Following

Once you join social media, be active. Engage followers so they don't get bored and leave!

Scripts and schedules can help organize content. Scripts outline what you'll say in a video. This makes filming easier. Schedules track what content you'll post and where. For example, every Friday you do highlight reels on YouTube. This sets follower expectations too, so they can look forward to highlight Fridays!

When setting schedules, be sure to pace yourself. Packed schedules can cause influencers to burn out. Instead, plan content ahead of time to help avoid stress and keep your followers interested.

Be safe and professional

Influencers may face online bullies and stalkers. What safety measures should you take? How much of your life story should you share with followers? Decide with an adult ahead of time. Never share your location or too much personal info.

Most social media platforms have built-in tools to help deal with bullies. These include the ability to block and report bullies, as well as to hide negative comments. Remember, bullying is against the rules. Bullies can lose their accounts, especially if more than one person reports them.

Similarly, don't make negative comments about other people or businesses online. You might hurt someone's feelings and lose followers. Hiring brands might not want to work with you. Bullying rules apply to you too, so always be polite and professional!

Online bullying, or cyberbullying, is never okay. Tell a trusted adult if you ever feel unsafe.

CHAPTER 3

MAKING MONEY

One way gaming influencers earn money is through social media. Some platforms let influencers attach adverts to their content. The influencer gets paid each time a follower views the ad. Some influencers make thousands of pounds! However, followers may run ad blockers, cutting this income stream.

Some platforms share **revenue** from product sales too. For instance, if a follower buys the game you're livestreaming, Twitch will split the revenue with you.

Influencers can also earn money from followers. Followers may pay monthly subscription fees to some influencer channels, especially for exclusive content. Followers and companies sometimes donate money. Influencers may also choose to sell products directly to their followers. They may open online shops to sell T-shirts, hats, games and more.

Selling clothing and other products with your logo can be a way to make money and advertise your brand.

Instead of money, influencers might receive free games or other products to try. They could even win a multi-million pound prize at an e-sports tournament or earn wages as a professional team player!

Fast Fact!

Team Liquid holds the world record for the most money won at e-sports contests. Teams in this pro gaming organization have played in more than 1,000 games and won close to £25 million.

Brand sponsorships

In the past, game makers and other brands hired ad companies to promote products. Now, influencers are often hired to create sponsored posts instead.

A sponsored post could be a photo of the brand's game on Instagram, a game review on YouTube and more. Sometimes the influencer even gets to test – and keep – a new game before it's available to the public! But successful influencers agree that they only work with brands they like and would use themselves.

As an influencer, you can partner with top brands to show off the latest games and consoles!

How do brands choose influencers? Brands look at your followers: how many you have, who they are and their engagement. Engagement is how many times a follower shares, likes, clicks or comments on content.

Some influencers cheat to make their engagement look better, though. They buy fake followers. They hire companies to run computer programs that view and like posts. Many brands now study follower engagement to catch cheating influencers – for them, it's game over!

Brands expect to earn more than what they spend on influencers. Micro-influencers and kidfluencers are cheaper to hire, and their followers are often more engaged. This means that the brand's **return on investment** is higher. For this reason, micro-influencers and kidfluencers are in demand! So don't worry if you don't have many followers.

Influencers are normally paid more for videos than shorter posts. Influencers' Instagram posts typically fetch about £100 for each post. This rises to about £750 per post if you have over 30,000 followers. Some brands pay an hourly rate instead and reimburse the influencer for money spent making the commercial. Other brands pay based on how engaged the influencer's followers are. Some brands forbid influencers from working with other brands at the same time, though. If this happens to you, try negotiating for more pay to make up for limiting your sources of income.

Ways to make money!

- Ad revenue
- Revenue share deals
- Brand sponsorships
- Follower subscriptions
- Donations
- Virtual tips
- E-sports prizes
- Online shop sales
- Freebies

Play by the rules

Let your followers know whether you were paid to post content or if a product you're using was free. The **Competition and Markets Authority** (CMA) requires it by law. This is because young children watching your channel may not understand the difference between a real reaction and a paid ad. Add the hashtag #ad or #sponsored at the start of a post or in a noticeable place. Don't bury the hashtag where someone may miss it. You also can't promote something you didn't try or like.

The CMA has other laws for social media. The Data Protection Act bans websites from collecting data from children without their permission from the age of 13. In response, YouTube might ban certain ads, turn off comments on childrens' sites and bury the sites in online searches. This could decrease influencer earnings.

Each country has its own child labour laws. Some countries want to apply these laws to online influencer jobs. In the United States, this includes requiring Coogan Accounts, which protect child income.

The Coogan Act

Child star Jackie Coogan lost his fortune to greedy adults. The Coogan Act shields child actors' wages. Fifteen per cent of their income must be put into a special bank account called a Coogan Account until the age of 18. A few states such as California have this law or a law like it. It doesn't include child influencers, but some lawmakers want to change this.

Jackie Coogan in a promotional image for the hit 1921 silent film, *The Kid*

Keep the coins flowing

There are many ways to make money as an influencer. But you will probably spend money as an influencer too. The costs may start to add up.

If you make more money than what you spend, congratulations! Your business is gaining money. This is called a profit. But if you spend more money than what you make each year, your business is losing money. This is called a loss. The difference between earnings and cost is the amount of profit or loss. The goal is to make a profit and prevent a loss.

A budget can help you keep track of your money. First, list all of your income. This is money earned. One day, your income might include ad revenue, brand sponsorships and more!

Fast Fact!

Piggy banks date all the way back to the 1300s! People have found ancient clay pots in the shape of boars with coins in them on the island of Java.

You can find free budget worksheets online to help track your money. You might need to hire an accountant to do it for you.

Next, decide how much to save. This is money you won't touch for everyday spending. Decide where to store your savings too. In a bank, money grows with **interest**. For example, you save £5,000 in a bank and it pays 5 per cent interest a year. After five years, you'll have £6,381. The bank paid you £1,381 for banking your money with them!

Finally, list the cost for each upcoming expense, including equipment. Taxes are also an expense. Each year, you must pay a part of your income to the government. Taxes must be paid on anything received for free as part of your work too.

CHAPTER 4

GROWING YOUR BUSINESS

Imagine how you'll feel when you get your first follower or first pay cheque! It won't be time to relax, though. You'll need to engage followers and build trust to grow your online community.

Be consistent and active so your followers stay with you. If you disappear, your followers will too. Respond to follower messages with the help of an adult. Each follower is potentially £1 in future income – more if they like, click, share and comment!

Study what leads to more engagement and followers. Most social media platforms provide tools to gather data. Put more effort into the kinds of posts that have more engagement. Better yet, ask your followers what they want to see. Consider the needs of everyone involved – including yourself. Being true to yourself builds trust with brands and your audience.

Keep your followers happy

Emotions can impact the market too. Happy people and happy times boost spending. So stay positive! As an influencer, you wield the power to steer a crowd. People often copy what a crowd does. This is called herd behaviour. People believe the group knows best, so they follow it, sometimes without knowing all the facts or making their own decisions. Influencing is based on herd behaviour.

Beware of exhausting your followers with endless ads. Many followers decide whether to buy a game the first time they see an ad. Three times fewer people buy the second time around. Don't annoy your followers by overselling!

Fast Fact!
Pop-up ads were created in the late 1990s. They are so disliked by internet users today that the inventor has apologized for making them!

More isn't always better. Too many ads or sponsored posts may drive away followers.

Beat the competition

More than half of young people want to be an influencer. The supply of influencers keeps growing. Will the demand for influencers keep growing too? Influencers drive supply. But followers, game makers and other brands drive demand, which is the desire for more influencers. As long as they want you, you can keep your influencing job.

When the demand for influencers is high, brands may be willing to pay influencers more. When the demand is low, brands may not pay as much. If there are more influencers (supply) than what brands need (demand), then the market is saturated. Influencers compete for fewer jobs.

Fast Fact!

Ancient people thought influence came from the stars. They believed it would drip down and change the way people behaved on Earth.

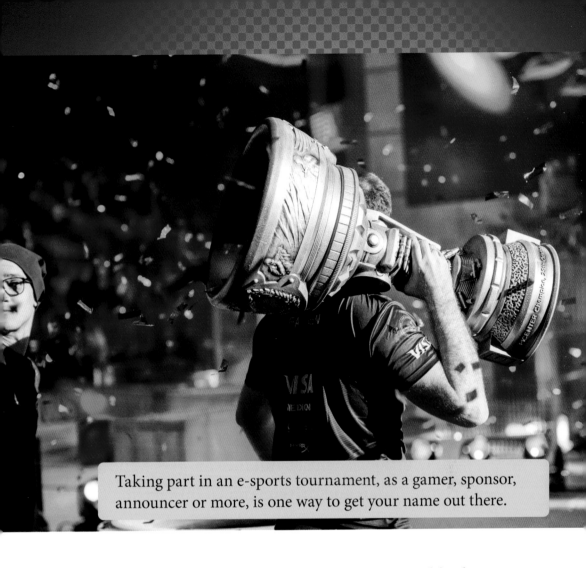

Taking part in an e-sports tournament, as a gamer, sponsor, announcer or more, is one way to get your name out there.

To win the game, you need to be more visible than the **competition**. Promote your sites through other influencers, bloggers and brands. Their followers may follow you and mention you to others. Hosting giveaways and contests can build your following too. Some influencers offer prizes in exchange for sharing posts with others.

Score big!

Gaming influencers play. But they also set trends, build communities and drive markets. Influencing can open new doors into designing video games, writing books and starting other businesses. But influencers must stay flexible. Technologies evolve. Laws and social media rules are growing stricter. Markets change.

What do you need to do to survive as an influencer? Be authentic. Be patient. Be consistent. But most of all, have fun! Game on!

Timeline

1950 — 1950s – First video games invented

1960 — 1960s – ARPANET invented

1970 — 1970s – First e-sports tournaments

1980

1983 – ARPANET opens to public as internet

1990

2000 — 2005 – First YouTube video posted

2010 — 2010 – Instagram started

2020 — 2011 – Twitch launched

GLOSSARY

agent person hired to make business deals for someone else

competition others in the same business you are in

Competition and Markets Authority UK government authority that makes sure businesses follow the law; abbreviated CMA

console special computer to play video games with a controller

copyright right by law to copy, sell, and publish a product or work

economics study of how goods and services are made, bought and sold

e-sports competitive video game playing

hashtag tag to group online posts and aid in searches; it starts with #

human capital value of a worker's skills towards meeting a goal

interest charge a borrower pays a lender

livestream online filming in present time

logo symbol meant to stand for a company

return on investment total of how much money you earn from something once how much you have spent on it is taken off

revenue money earned from sales

social media websites people use to share content

FIND OUT MORE

BOOKS

E-sports Revolution (Video Game Revolution), Daniel Mauleón (Raintree, 2020)

Making YouTube Videos: Star in Your Own Video!, Nick Willoughby (For Dummies, 2019)

Paid to Game (Video Game Revolution), Daniel Mauleón (Raintree, 2020)

Understanding Social Media (Decoding Media Literacy), Pamela Dell (Raintree, 2019).

WEBSITES

influencermatchmaker.co.uk/blog/kid-influencers-meet-next-generation-social-media-stars
Find out about some of the most successful 'kidfluencers'.

www.bbc.co.uk/newsround/49822698
Read more about kidfluencers at CBBC Newsround.

INDEX